★ JUSTICE ★

★★★★★★ JUSTICE ★★★★★

BY JOAN JOHNSON

An American Values First Book
FRANKLIN WATTS 1985
New York/London/Toronto/Sydney

Photographs courtesy of:
Bettmann Archive: pp. 9, 16, 22;
AP/Wide World Photos: pp. 34, 43, 46;
Conklin/Monkmeyer Press, Inc.: p. 50;
Supreme Court Historical Society: p. 60.

Library of Congress Cataloging in Publication Data

Johnson, Joan (Joan J.)
Justice.

(An American values first book)
Includes index.
Summary: Explores the development, strengths, and
weaknesses of the American system of justice and the
meaning of due process of law and the rights of the
accused.
1. Criminal justice, Administration of—United States
—History—Juvenile literature. 2. Criminal procedure—
United States—History—Juvenile literature. 3. Due
process of law—United States—History—Juvenile literature. [1. Criminal justice, Administration of—History.
2. Criminal procedure—History. 3. Due process of law—
History] I. Title. II. Series.
KF9223.Z9J64 1985   345.73'05   85-5404
ISBN 0-531-10043-X   347.3055

★★★★

CONTENTS

★ JUSTICE ★

★ 1 ★

WHAT IS
JUSTICE?

Juan Perez hurried down the front steps of his apartment building. He was late. His friend Julio was waiting for him at the gym five blocks away. He broke into a run, worrying that Julio might leave without him.

At that moment, a police car turned the corner. The officers knew that moments before a robbery and murder had occurred at a nearby grocery store. One male suspect wearing a worn dungaree jacket, black pants, and leather boots had been seen fleeing. The officers both spotted Juan at the same time. Juan's description matched that of the suspect.

Sure that Juan was their man, they slammed their car to a halt and leaped out to arrest him. Juan offered no resistance. After being searched, handcuffed, and read his rights, he willingly climbed into the squad car.

On the way to the police station, he tried to explain that he was running only because he was late. The officers did not believe him. Instead they pulled him from the car and led him into the stationhouse. As they walked toward the main desk, a woman pointed at Juan and cried, "That's him! He's the one!"

Juan knew he was in serious trouble.

In that same city on that same morning, Will Stone, a wealthy account manager, parked his Cadillac and strode into his office. He was surprised to see his boss and a stranger standing by his desk. He knew instinctively that the agency had finally caught on. He had been siphoning money from clients' accounts and they now knew.

Drawing himself up to look innocently surprised, he smiled and said, "Something the matter?"

His boss eyed him disgustedly. "Will, this is Detective Gainor. He has a warrant for your arrest. You have some explaining to do."

Both Juan and Will had come face to face with the American justice system. For the next few months or even years, both would wish they hadn't. Both were accused of serious crimes. Juan, of course, was innocent. But Juan came from a poor family. His parents had immigrated to the United States twelve years before. His father was disabled and his mother worked as a seamstress to support her family. Juan's family was poor and had little knowledge of their rights as American citizens.

Will's case was different. Will was a millionaire. He knew powerful people, even state senators and members of Con-

Perfect justice requires absolute equality before the law, as illustrated in this woodcut of the Roman allegorical figure Justicia.

gress. Will was guilty, but he intended to avoid punishment for his crime. Before he'd answer any of Detective Gainor's questions, he called his personal lawyer, one of the most famous in the state. His lawyer immediately came to the office to see that none of Will's rights were abused.

Juan and Will were from the same city. They were of different ages and importance in their communities. One was poor, the other rich. What happened to each of them is what our system of justice is about. Did Will stand a better chance of avoiding punishment for a crime he committed than Juan did for a crime he knew nothing about? How was Juan to protect himself when neither he nor his family knew very much at all about our justice system? When they could not even afford a lawyer?

Answers to these questions are not easy ones. No one could ensure that Juan would be found innocent or that Will would not go free after stealing thousands of dollars from clients. But that is the aim of our justice system.

Justice defines our rights within the limits of our Constitution and our Bill of Rights. It also defines crime. Justice prevents abuse of individuals by their government or by other individuals. It protects and it punishes. It must be even-handed, so that all people are treated equally, no matter how poor or how wealthy they are. And it imposes limits on the government, the police, and the courts, by ensuring that certain procedures are followed when an individual is accused of a crime.

The police are sure Juan robbed and killed the grocery store clerk. Our justice system, however, will require that they prove their case against Juan. It will provide Juan with a lawyer, called a public defender, to protect Juan's rights and see to it that he gets a fair trial. Before Juan even faces trial, other procedures will require the police to prove they have enough evidence to justify trying him.

In Will's case, our justice system will do everything it can to prove his guilt and see to it that he is punished. Justice demands that the public be protected from people like Will.

How this happens and why, the strengths of our justice system and its weaknesses, how our concept of justice developed, the meaning of such terms as "due process of law" and the "rights of the accused" are the subject of this book.

★ 2 ★

HOW THE CONCEPT OF JUSTICE DEVELOPED

Early humankind's idea of justice was simple. They needed food for survival. If a man chased and killed a beast, the meat was his. If anyone else tried to steal his meat, he had to fight, even to the death. Early people owned no property. They traveled for food. Because they were on the move, they had few possessions.

Early people did not consider themselves very important in their world. Their lives were often in danger. Survival was everything. Early justice meant that anyone or anything that threatened a person's survival had to be chased away or killed.

Early people began living in groups because groups made survival easier. Many people could fight off enemies better than one. Many could work together to hunt meat. But living in groups created new problems. Arguments had to be settled. Rights to belongings had to be established. Violence among group members could not be tolerated. A dead man left a family that the group then had to support. To function, the group had to provide safety. So rules were made. Everyone was expected to follow them. These were not written rules. Writing had not yet developed. These were oral rules, sometimes called taboos, that were passed down from parents to children, generation after generation.

Enforcing the rules made it necessary to develop punishments. Punishment made an example of the wrongdoer. It discouraged others from breaking the rules. Sometimes if one person murdered another, he was given the responsibility of the dead person's family, even when he already had one of his own. Another punishment was death. In some ways, even worse than death was exile from the tribe. The wrongdoer was sent away. He lost the protection of the tribe. He had to survive alone, the easy victim of hungry beasts or hostile strangers.

When disputes arose, a chief was needed to settle them. He had to know all the rules. He had to have the power to decide who had broken the rules. He had to decide what the punishment would be. He was the judge and the jury. Justice, then, depended on this leader's wisdom and fairness.

A good chief's main concern was the group, the harmony and the safety of the group. Anyone who threatened group safety or harmony had to be punished. The rights of the "wrongdoer" were of little or no importance. Even if he was innocent, his individual fate was of little matter.

EARLY CIVILIZATIONS
AND WRITTEN LAW

Later, as early humankind learned to plant food rather than traveling to find it, these groups grew into civilizations. These were complex, highly sophisticated societies. They developed writing, which they did on stone or clay tablets.

Once writing developed, many early rulers ordered that the laws, so long passed down by word of mouth, be recorded. The first known written laws were ordered by Hammurabi sometime between 1950 and 1850 B.C. Other societies followed. The Hebrew Torah is dated from around 1,000 B.C., and work on the written Talmud began around 500 B.C. Solon (639 to 559 B.C.) became the great Greek lawmaker. All of these systems of law established that rules are necessary for people to live peaceably together and that punishments would be imposed on those who broke them. They also made clear exactly what was a crime and what was not. Because the laws were written, rulers could not easily change them to suit selfish needs. The people, at least those who could read, could point to their laws when they wanted justice.

JUSTICE FOR
THE INDIVIDUAL

Although written laws were a step toward greater justice for every person, they were only a first step. Many great people, among them Mohammed, Buddha, and Jesus, taught that all human beings were important in God's eyes. They had rights given them by God. The Greeks, believing in the dignity and importance of human beings, developed a society in which all citizens had a voice in their government and the right to be protected from unjust rulers. A person's sense of importance and worth in his world grew.

Greek lawmaker Solon dictates his system of law to Athenian scribes.

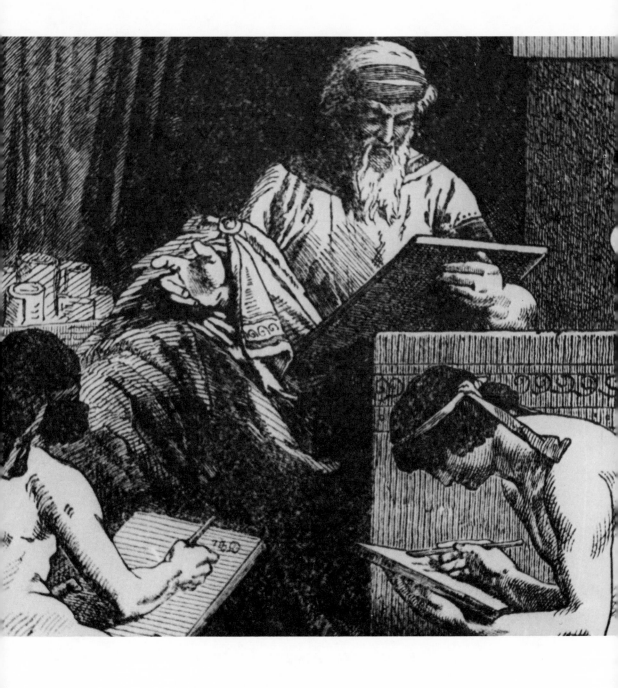

Yet the rights of the common person still took centuries to develop. Throughout most of our history, the common person has been mistreated by those in power—chiefs, kings, and dictators.

Even today, the strong and the powerful in some societies rob him of his property or jail him or put him to death without concern for his rights. In some present-day societies, dictators protect their power and that of a select few by maintaining order—peace—without regard for the rights of the individual. Justice for all is not important.

BALANCING THE RIGHTS OF THE INDIVIDUAL AND THE GROUP

Other societies have slowly, but steadily, increased the rights of each citizen and limited the power of the select few. Yet these societies still manage to keep peace and order. They protect the group, but they also protect the one, the lone individual, because both are important. Every decision that is made, every law that is passed, must take both the needs of the group and the rights of the individual into consideration. This is no easy task. Sometimes protecting the group would be easier if the rights of the individual could be ignored. Sometimes concern for the welfare of the individual seems to endanger the welfare of the group. But true justice can exist only in societies that always attempt to balance both the rights of the group and the rights of the lone citizen within the group.

In the United States, it is easy to take our rights and freedoms for granted. Yet winning these rights and freedoms was no easy task. Continuing to balance the importance of the group and the rights of each citizen is an ongoing process. That process was begun centuries ago. If we study the growing importance of the individual and the growth of real justice, we see that the two go hand in hand.

★ 3 ★

THE EARLY
BRITISH SYSTEM
OF JUSTICE

Much of our American system of justice was adapted from England's. Today England is a free society. Yet it wasn't always. England was once ruled by kings and queens who had complete power over the lives of their subjects. Kings and queens believed they had been given "divine right" of power by God. Their word was not to be questioned. Their goal was to protect royalty from anything or anyone who threatened it. Any attempt by a common person to "demand his rights" or "demand justice" was a threat to that power.

Early English justice meant maintaining order. It was called "the king's peace." This makes clear exactly for whose benefit order was kept. The lone citizen had no importance at all. His or her rights to protection from the government or from criminals were limited. This is reflected in the two most common forms of justice that existed before 1215. One was the blood feud; the other was hanging. They were common in the 600s and 700s. Both were violent and neither required weighing the facts fairly to prevent mistreatment of innocent people.

THE BLOOD FEUD

The blood feud was carried on between families. If a family member was injured or killed, his survivors were obligated to get even. They caught and killed their relative's murderer. But then the murderer's survivors were obligated to get even. An endless string of revenge killings began, sometimes wiping out whole families.

HANGING OR LYNCHING

If a crime was committed, perhaps a theft, and someone witnessed the theft, he cried out, "Thief!" The thief would run, closely pursued by anyone who heard the shout. It was everyone's moral obligation to chase the thief. Even if the thief made it to the next town, new pursuers took up the chase until he was cornered. Judgment was made on the spot. More than likely a rope was strung over a tree limb and the thief was hanged. Afterward, everyone would feel good about what they had done. They had all participated in preserving order. Few, if any, would go home uneasy about their actions. It was, in fact, a favorite event in the lives of those who lived in the seventh and eighth centuries. Yet hanging was mob violence. It was brutal. It gave no thought to the individual.

DEALING WITH DOUBT—
COMPURGATION, ORDEAL,
AND TRIAL BY BATTLE

By the ninth and tenth centuries, the British had developed three additional forms of justice. Each was meant to cope with the problem of doubt. Justice was one thing when the criminal was caught in the act. But often, a crime was not witnessed or the victim did not live to tell about it. In such cases, accusations were made. If a person denied guilt, he could sometimes prove innocence through "compurgation."

Only a wealthy person could use compurgation. A nobleman would bring to a hearing several people who, in a formal statement, said, "He said he was innocent and he wouldn't lie." They were not witnesses. They did not state the accused was with them at the time of the crime. They did not actually see the crime committed. They gave no evidence. They didn't even refer to the crime. They merely recited a memorized statement about the accused person's honesty. If anyone forgot his lines or slipped on a word or failed to be convincing, the accused would be found guilty. If the accused had gathered enough people who recited well, he was found innocent.

The reasoning behind compurgation was that a person of good reputation was less likely a criminal than a person of poor reputation. But the practice could be used only when the person accused of the crime was richer or more powerful than the accuser. Unfortunately, this allowed a wealthy noble to literally "get away with murder" as long as he murdered someone poorer or less powerful than he.

Compurgation was used for many centuries, and not legally stopped in England until 1883. In Colonial America, white settlers used something like it to clear themselves of charges brought by Indians. Blacks have had it used to deny them justice in many southern courts. Our modern-day practice of calling in "character witnesses," people who testify about the honesty and goodness of the person on trial, traces back to compurgation. The only thing that can be said in favor of compurgation is that at least it protected the innocent better than the blood feud and hanging.

Ordeal was the second process developed for proving innocence when doubt existed. Ordeal was a supernatural test. The results supposedly were a sign from God. With ordeal, the people did not have to make any weighty decisions about the accused's guilt or innocence and so could not be responsible if they were wrong. Had Juan Perez lived in those times, when he denied his guilt he would have been forced to carry a hot iron in his bare hands or dip his arm in boiling water. If his burn healed well and quickly, he'd go free. If instead the burn became infected, Juan would be put to death. Another test was ordeal by water. Juan's arms and legs would be bound tightly. He would then be thrown in a river or lake. The people believed that water accepted the innocent, rejected or floated the guilty. If Juan floated, he was guilty. If he sank, he was innocent. If the townspeople pulled him out before he drowned, Juan would live. If he drowned before they pulled him out, the people felt that at least he would be sure of a place in heaven.

Ordeal was formally abolished in England in the 1200s. It, too, was a popular pastime to witness. But because ordeal depended on a sign from God, the "trial" required the presence of a priest. In the 1200s the Church of England refused to participate any longer. The practice began to die out. It did not, however, die completely. The Puritans in Colonial America used ordeal by water four centuries later.

Trial by battle was less popular than by ordeal. If Will's boss had decided that Will had stolen from his company and Will denied the charge, they would have had to meet on the battlefield. Supposedly, God determined the winner in trial by battle. Yet the audience could see that the winner was the

better fighter. Trial by battle lacked magic. Its outcome was determined by skill, not a supernatural sign.

Since trial by battle required that the accuser and the victim (or his survivors) fight, if the criminal was bigger, stronger, or a more skilled fighter, often the wise victim decided not to bring charges. It was better to forget the incident than to risk one's life. Thus, if Will's boss thought he might lose the fight, he might never report Will's crime. Will would be free to steal again. Justice, protection and punishment, would not exist. These five forms of British justice show little regard for the rights of the individual, especially the rights of the common people. Justice was keeping peace, order, and the power of nobles and kings. Citizens often had to get justice for themselves through the blood feud, hanging, or trial by battle.

Any person, no matter how honest, could easily find himself accused of a crime. Often the accused person had no chance to prove his innocence—he might be hanged by an angry mob without any chance to speak. Even if one did have a chance to deny guilt, proving innocence through ordeal was itself a punishment. Many died trying.

Making the punishment fit the crime was not important. Many minor crimes were punishable by death. Yet those who were wealthy or powerful, the nobles, could abuse the rights of lesser citizens without fear of punishment. Many

In this drawing a medieval woman accused of witchcraft is forced to walk across red-hot plowshares (a type of shovel) as her trial by ordeal.

★ 17 ★

used compurgation's memorized speeches to recite away the honest charges against them. And if the king or a noble decided he wanted to get rid of a troublesome person, that person could be tumbled into jail without any real charges and with no chance to prove his innocence. When the individual didn't count, justice did not exist.

★ 4 ★

TOWARD A
TRUER CONCEPT
OF JUSTICE

Some societies believe in the importance of the individual. They believe human beings have value and dignity. These societies have the strongest and most meaningful system of justice. Our United States Constitution was founded on democratic ideals. It values justice and freedom above all else. But our system of justice did not spring, fully developed, from the minds of our forebears. As we saw in the last chapter, justice before the twelfth century wasn't very just at all. Before our Constitution and Bill of Rights could be written, many things had to happen. Changes had to be made, not only in the ways governments were organized but also in the ways people thought.

THE CLARENDON JURY

In 1166, England's King Henry created the Clarendon Jury. Unhappy with the hangings, the blood feuds, compurgation, and trial by ordeal or battle, Henry sent his officers to act as jurors in the villages. When a charge against someone had been made, they asked questions of the people of the village. Finally, if they believed the charges were fair, they prepared a report saying that a particular person was believed to have committed a crime. That person then faced trial by ordeal.

The importance of Henry's jury in the development of justice is twofold. Some historians compare the Clarendon Jury with our modern-day grand jury, which hears the facts in a case to decide whether enough evidence against the accused exists to justify a trial. More important, however, once the Clarendon Jury accused someone of a crime, the sentence was banishment from England *even if* he passed the ordeal. Ordeal was no longer the supreme test. A criminal who passed the ordeal was still punished. Society was rid of him. And for the first time, guilt or innocence rested not on the chance of a burn healing or a body sinking in water, but on people using their minds to weigh facts.

THE MAGNA CHARTA

Many historians believe that the common people's need for justice and a fair say in their government began to be met in England in 1215. That year the nobles of King John forced him to sign the famous Magna Charta. They felt that he had deprived them of their rights. They wanted a signed promise that the king would honor their rights to property and would treat them justly. They also demanded the right to be judged by only their equals, no one of lower station. That promise became the basis for trial by a jury of equals.

Later British kings and nobles began to lose more and more power to the common person. Merchants and business-men set up Parliament to advise the king. Soon Parliament began to take on many decision-making powers. King John's noblemen had had no intention of protecting the rights of the common people in their "jury of peers" clause. Yet years later it was used by the common person to obtain justice in disputes with nobles. A noble hearing his case was likely to protect the special privileges of the noble class. By demanding that their case be heard by others of their own class, their own peers, average citizens stood a far better chance for justice.

THE ENGLISH
BILL OF RIGHTS

Although King John signed the Magna Charta in 1215, British kings four centuries later were still trying to regain the absolute power they once had. In 1628, King Charles I forced the issue once again. By this time, however, Parliament had become stronger. It raised an army of the people and forced the king to sign another famous agreement, the Petition of Right. As did the Magna Charta, this document required the king to respect rights. This time, however, the rights were the people's. When he later broke his promise, a war ensued. Charles lost and was brought to trial. Found guilty, he was beheaded. Never had anything like this occurred. The power of the people over their ruler was clear. When later another king, James II, tried once more to regain absolute power, he was removed from the throne. In 1689 Parliament forced the next rulers, William and Mary, to sign several documents before they could reign. The Bill of Rights accepted Parliament's absolute power and outlined British citizens' rights to own property, to write and say what they wanted, and when accused of a crime, to expect fair treatment.

The signing of the Constitution, which,
with the Amendments, provides the
legal foundation for justice in America.

THE AMERICAN
CONSTITUTION

Nearly a century later, when such famous men as George Washington, James Madison, and Alexander Hamilton met in 1787 to draw up our Constitution, they were well aware that a strong government was necessary to protect citizens from abuse of their rights. They were also certain that the government must be set up so that no one person or group could grab power and use it for personal ends. They wanted to limit the power of this new government so that the rights of the individual were protected.

The Constitution made clear that no citizen could be put in jail without an explanation. In it the Writ of Habeas Corpus required that anyone being held in jail be brought before a judge. He would then determine whether the evidence justified trial or whether the prisoner should be released. Another important section forbade the government to pass any law that took away a citizen's property, freedom, or life. Those punishments could be imposed only after the person had a fair trial. The Constitution also made it illegal to punish a person for committing a crime that was not recognized as a crime when it was committed, to change the penalty for a crime after it had been committed, or to alter laws to make it easier to convict someone accused of a crime.

★ 5 ★

THE AMERICAN
BILL
OF RIGHTS

The Constitution defined the government in such a way that no one branch of the government could assume complete power. Still, many people were worried that this system of "checks and balances" might not be enough to ensure all the rights citizens deserved. The Bill of Rights was ratified in 1791. It contained ten amendments to the Constitution. They clearly defined exactly what rights a citizen had and limited the power of the government over its people. All of the amendments are important—the rights to freedom of religion, freedom of speech, freedom of the press, freedom to peaceably assemble, and the right to keep and bear arms. But certain amendments determined the kind of justice Americans could expect.

THE FOURTH AMENDMENT

Our forebears were well aware of misuses of power by governing royalty. Many English kings and queens had abused their subjects' right to privacy by having soldiers enter their homes to search for evidence to use against them. The Fourth Amendment forbids such practices. It protects citizens from unreasonable searches and/or seizures of their persons, houses, papers, and effects.

The difficulty with the Fourth Amendment is in the word "unreasonable." For the nearly two hundred years that have passed since the ratification of the Bill of Rights, the definition of "unreasonable" has been the source of much argument.

Today, police searches must be conducted according to set procedures. First, the police must get a "search warrant" signed by a judge. The judge will not allow the search unless the police have "probable cause," or good reason, to believe that criminal activity or illegal articles will be found. They cannot conduct a general search. The police must describe specifically which places will be searched and the articles they believe they will find. Once the warrant is obtained, however, the police may do whatever is necessary to conduct their search, even if they must break down a door.

New inventions have caused many problems in protecting people from unreasonable searches. It is one thing to search a home or an office for things such as files, money, or stolen articles. But what of invading privacy by listening in on phone conversations? Phone-tapping devices were used to gather evidence against many people suspected of crimes until the Supreme Court, in 1967, made the practice illegal. A year later Congress passed a law that permitted the use of wiretapping when used for national security if a court order is obtained first.

In comparison to other kinds of search warrants, wire- or phone-tapping warrants are very difficult to obtain. Only state or federal judges may authorize them. No law exists, however, that requires police to get warrants before using "undercover" measures such as hiding cameras or tape recorders on themselves. They can also listen in on phone extensions when they have permission from one of the people involved.

Seizure means that the police restrain a person's freedom of movement by physical force or by a show of authority. That person does not feel he is free to leave. Legally seizing or arresting a person also has certain requirements. For instance, the police are forbidden to enter someone's home to arrest him unless they have a warrant. They may enter without a warrant only if they have good reason to believe a life-threatening situation exists. In public places, arrests can be made without a warrant if police believe they have "probable cause"—strong indications that the person has just committed or is about to commit a crime. If they do arrest without a warrant, however, the accused person must be brought before a judge immediately afterward. The judge will then decide whether the arrest was justified.

THE FIFTH AMENDMENT

The Fifth Amendment requires the government to present its evidence against someone accused of a serious crime to a *grand jury* before it can actually try a person in court. A grand jury is usually composed of twelve to twenty-three citizens. These jurors hear the evidence, but they do not decide whether the accused person is guilty or innocent. They merely decide whether enough evidence has been gathered against the accused to justify a trial.

The designers of the Bill of Rights knew all too well how easily kings had leveled charges against honest citizens. The Fifth Amendment requirement forces the government to be extremely careful and thorough with regard to the charges it brings against citizens. It puts the burden on the government to have strong evidence, a good case against someone, before formally charging that person.

Another part of the Fifth Amendment declares that once a person has been found innocent of a crime, he cannot be tried again for that same crime. He is free forever, even if new evidence is found. This clause has two purposes. On the one hand, it prevents government from "going after a person," as kings and queens did in England when they were determined to put an enemy in jail. Sometimes a British subject was found innocent, only to be re-charged with the same crime later. Under such circumstances, no one could ever "go on" with his life. The dark possibility that he could again be charged loomed on the horizon. This section of the Fifth Amendment prohibits that possibility.

The Fifth Amendment also ensures that the accused has the right to remain silent. No person who stands trial for criminal charges can be forced to testify against himself. No assumption of guilt can be drawn from refusal to testify. It is not the accused's responsibility to prove his innocence; it is the government's responsibility to prove guilt. The government must be able to do so without the accused's testimony. If the accused person does choose to take the stand, he cannot then claim the right to remain silent when questioned by the prosecutor. Although this right was originally intended for criminal prosecutions, it has been used regularly by people questioned in congressional hearings and other government investigations.

One of the most confusing provisions of the Fifth Amendment is that which states that no one can be deprived of life, liberty, or property without "due process of law."

"Due process," however, seems to have no exact definition, and even the Supreme Court refuses to define it precisely.

Due process requires, for instance, that all laws be clear in meaning and application. If they are vague, they violate due process. Due process requires certain procedures by which a case is heard. Due process requires that all provisions of the Bill of Rights in the Fourth through Eighth amendments are observed in all court cases. It tries to ensure fairness.

Due process refers not only to how the government may use its power, but it also limits when and why that power may be exercised. It protects us against unreasonable laws, no matter how clearly defined or properly enacted they are. Confining mentally ill people against their wishes if they are not dangerous to themselves or the public, for instance, is an unreasonable limit of their liberty. It violates due process. Even if a law reflects the wishes of the majority, it must also be a reasonable law. It must be just.

THE SIXTH AMENDMENT

The Sixth Amendment deals with the rights of those accused of crimes. First of all, those accused of a crime have a right to a "speedy" trial. How quickly the trial actually occurs after arrest, however, is affected by several things. Those accused of crimes often ask for many delays in order to prepare their cases. Delays often work to benefit the defendants because people forget and their testimony grows foggier. The court's schedule of cases, called a *docket*, is also crowded. It may be a long time before an opening occurs. But the government is obligated to at least state in advance the time limits for bringing the case to trial. Should a reasonable "speedy trial" be denied, the case must be dismissed.

The trial may not be held in secret; it must be public. The accused has the right to a jury drawn from the state and district in which the crime was supposedly committed. The Constitution allows state courts to have juries composed of at least six people who, by majority, decide the defendant's guilt. Federal courts are required to have a jury of twelve people who must *all* agree that the defendant is guilty. To be impartial, juries must be a fair cross-section of the community.

The defendant also has the right to be sure that each member of the jury has no prejudice against him because of race, religion or national origin. His attorney can question possible jurors before the trial and excuse those whose decisions might be unfairly influenced by prejudice.

No one can be held in jail without being informed of the charges against him or her. If there are witnesses against the accused, he or she has the right to confront those witnesses and challenge their testimonies. He also has the right to force into court witnesses who can help his case, even if they do not want to testify. Last, the accused has the right to have a lawyer to protect his rights, to prepare the defense, and to present the case in court.

THE SEVENTH AMENDMENT

The Sixth Amendment protects the defendant's right to a trial by jury when charged with a crime. The Seventh Amendment protects the right to a trial for those sued in civil cases. Civil cases are different from criminal cases. Criminal cases involve such crimes as assault, kidnapping, theft, or murder. In civil cases, no crime has been committed, yet some "harm" or "injury" has been done. Perhaps one person has written untrue things about another. Perhaps someone has failed to live up to an agreement with another. In some but not all civil cases, those sued have the right to a trial by jury.

THE EIGHTH AMENDMENT

The Eighth Amendment protects those accused of crimes and those found guilty of crimes in three ways. In early times people accused of crimes often had to wait in jail until their cases came to court. They had not yet been proven guilty. They actually might have been innocent. Being jailed while awaiting trial was an unjust punishment. They should have had the right to remain free until found guilty. Some way to ensure their return at the time of trial had to be devised. It is called "bail." Bail is a bond or guarantee of payment should the accused person disappear before his trial. A judge sets the amount of bail required to free an accused person until the time of trial. Bail can be very high if the crime is considered quite serious or if the accused person is not very reliable. The Eighth Amendment, however, forbids federal judges to set excessively high bail.

Sometimes, as in cases involving very serious crimes such as murder, judges may refuse to release a defendant, even if he can pay bail. The reason is that a defendant who could be put to death for his crimes would be likely to run no matter how high the bail. Judges also have the right to release defendants without bail if they are reliable members of the community. Fines are often part or all of the punishment chosen by the judge. The Eighth Amendment protects the guilty from excessive fines.

The Eighth Amendment protects those found guilty of crimes from "cruel or unusual punishment." In early America, punishments for many crimes were unnecessarily harsh. The death penalty was imposed for many non-serious crimes. Many people today believe that the death penalty is too cruel, so it is used only under very limited circumstances.

JUSTICE AS A PROCESS

The Bill of Rights did much to protect people from abuse by the government, especially those accused of crimes. It is the basis of our justice system. But it was not the final step in the development of true justice in the United States. Other amendments were later added to the Constitution. For example, the Fourteenth Amendment requires that laws in the individual states protect the right to due process of law. In addition, new interpretations of the meaning of the Bill of Rights have developed as new situations have arisen. The meaning of such terms as "due process" has been altered several times in the two hundred years that have passed since the Bill of Rights was enacted. More change based on new interpretations will occur. True and perfect justice may never be possible, but in the United States, our desire for justice means that the process must continue.

★ 6 ★

THE RIGHTS
OF THE ACCUSED
AT ARREST

Juan and Will came face to face with the American justice system on the same morning. From the moment the police made contact with them, they could expect and demand certain rights. These protections were outlined in our Constitution and Bill of Rights, and supported by later amendments and new interpretations of constitutional rights. All of these factors determined how justly Juan and Will would be treated from the time of their arrest to the time when their cases were either dropped or they were found innocent, or they had been punished and set free.

WARRANTS FOR ARREST
AND FOR SEARCH

When Will walked into his office, his boss and Detective Gainor were already prepared to serve him with two warrants. The first was a search warrant that the detective had secured from the court. It authorized him to search Will's belongings at his office and his home for letters or files. Will's boss had made a complaint that Will's clients' accounts were several thousand dollars short. The second warrant was for his arrest. The detective had sworn, under oath, that there was "probable cause," or good reason, to believe Will had stolen money from his clients.

The officers who arrested Juan, on the other hand, had no warrants. Juan was on a public street, his description matched that of a suspect seen running from the grocery store, and he was running at the time. The officers had probable cause to believe that Juan had just committed the crime. They arrested him.

THE RIGHT TO REMAIN SILENT AND THE RIGHT TO AN ATTORNEY

The Fifth Amendment does much to protect defendants' rights. It prevents the police from getting confessions through torture or what came to be known as "the third degree." In 1964 in the case of *Escobedo* v. *Illinois*, the Supreme Court ruled that confessions obtained when the defendant has been refused the right to an attorney cannot be used in court. Two years later, in the case of *Miranda* v. *Arizona*, the Supreme Court gave defendants even greater protection. It ruled that defendants must be informed of their right to remain silent, to have an attorney present, and to have the court hire an attorney if they cannot afford one. This is called "the Miranda Warning" and it must be read to the arrested person before any questioning occurs. Both Will and Juan were read their rights at the moment of their arrest. Will immediately called his lawyer. Juan was held without

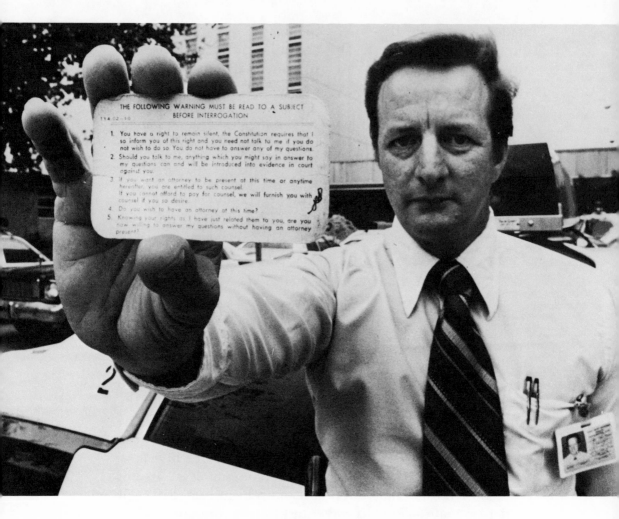

A Dade County, Florida, police officer displays the Miranda warning. Since the 1966 Supreme Court ruling in Miranda v. Arizona, *police officers are required to read these rights to a suspect before questioning can begin.*

questioning at the police station until a public defender was appointed to represent him.

THE PUBLIC DEFENDER

Anyone accused of a crime in the United States has always had the right to a lawyer if he or she could afford one. Many could not. Thus a poor person stood less chance of justice because he could not afford an expert to guide him. In 1938, in the trial of *Johnson* v. *Zerbst,* one step was taken toward greater justice. The Court ruled that in all federal trials, defendants have the right to an attorney appointed by the Court if they are too poor to pay for one themselves. In 1963, in the case of *Gideon* v. *Wainwright,* it was further ruled that in state trials, anyone subject to questioning had the same right. In 1972, the Supreme Court specified that in any case in which conviction could mean a prison sentence, a defendant had the right to a public defender. Juan needed a public defender because his family could not afford a private attorney. Someone from the public defenders' office was immediately called in to consult with Juan. Will, of course, hired a top-notch private lawyer from a well-known firm. He wanted special attention and knew that he would need the best possible lawyer if he was ever to beat the charges against him.

THE FIRST CONTACT
WITH A JUDGE

Soon both Will and Juan stood before a district judge who restated their rights to silence and a lawyer. The record must clearly show that those accused of crimes were aware of these rights. Otherwise, any proceedings against them can be held unconstitutional. The judge then set Will's bail at $20,000. This was not excessive considering Will's wealth. The judge refused, however, to set bail for Juan. He felt that since Juan had been accused of armed robbery and murder, no amount of money could ensure that, once free, Juan would return for his trial. He ordered Juan held in the city jail until the grand jury heard the evidence against him.

Will paid a professional bail bondsman the ten percent fee required—$2,000—and the bail bondsman posted Will's bail. That meant that if Will ran away, the bail bondsman would have to pay the government $20,000. Will was released with orders to remain in the district until a grand jury convened to hear his case.

★ 7 ★

JUSTICE
BETWEEN ARREST
AND TRIAL

Juan and Will could expect certain rights at the time of their arrest. But many other factors in their cases would also have a bearing on whether they received due process, justice, before their trials.

THE PROSECUTOR

The prosecutor represents the People or the government. First he decides whether the police have enough evidence to support charges against a defendant. Then he decides which charges to make. He then prepares the government's case and presents that case to a grand jury. If successful in convincing the jury that the evidence justifies a trial, he argues the case in court.

The prosecutor's job is to weigh both sides of the case before proceeding. Trying innocent citizens is not his goal. If he doubts that the charges against a defendant can be supported, if he has any doubt that the accused person is guilty, he will probably drop the charges. At some point before cases reach the courtroom, nearly half are dropped.

Sometimes a prosecutor will decide to charge a defendant with a lesser crime, a crime which is not as serious and which has lighter penalties. He may do this because the serious charges have penalties he thinks unjust for that particular case. Or he may decide that proving the graver charges would be too difficult. He may also make a deal with the defendant's attorney. He will charge the defendant with a lesser crime if the defendant will agree to plead guilty.

PLEA BARGAINING

Ninety percent of all convictions are the result of guilty pleas. Almost all of those guilty pleas result from plea bargaining. Will's lawyer contacted the prosecutor's office. He hoped the prosecutor would be interested in lowering the charges against Will, so that he would serve little or no time in prison. Will's lawyer recognized that proving him innocent was next to impossible, for Will had not been careful about disguising certain bank deposits he made with stolen money. He knew the prosecutor would use this as strong evidence against Will. The prosecutor did consider the offer, but in going over the evidence his office had obtained against Will, he decided his case was good and that Will should be punished. Juan's case, however, bothered him. Except for the one witness against Juan, a lot of the evidence seemed doubtful. The gun that had been used to kill the grocery clerk had not been found, nor was it on Juan when he was arrested. The time between the crime and Juan's arrest was a little too short. Other things bothered him. He knew this would be a difficult case to prove, so he offered to plea bargain with Juan. Juan's lawyer explained that with lesser charges, Juan might have to serve only a few years. If Juan refused to bargain and was found guilty, the penalty could be death. He told Juan it would be safer to plead guilty to lesser charges, but Juan knew he was innocent. Even though he was fearful of being found guilty, he refused.

Many people criticize the use of plea bargaining. Often criminals who should have served twenty or thirty years are released after only three or four because they "copped a plea," or plea bargained. But often, plea bargaining is a useful tool. Often the more serious charges against a defendant might not be provable to a jury beyond a reasonable doubt. A guilty person could go free. At least with plea bargaining some punishment is suffered. And plea bargaining makes the justice system more efficient. No lengthy trial is needed when the defendant pleads guilty. The prosecutor's office is free to pursue other cases and the court docket is cleared so that other cases come to trial sooner.

THE GRAND JURY

Having prepared his cases, the prosecutor presented the evidence against both Will and Juan to twenty-three men and women. The grand jury was not required to decide whether either defendant was guilty or innocent. They merely heard the evidence. Neither Juan nor Will had the right to appear before the grand jury unless the jury ordered or invited them to appear. Neither were. Having heard the evidence, the grand jury decided by majority vote that both cases should be brought to trial. They issued a true bill, or *indictment*, for both Will and Juan. It stated the nature of the crimes for which they were being charged.

THE SECOND TIME
BEFORE A JUDGE

After the grand jury returned its indictment against Will, the judge doubled his bail. Both Will's and Juan's defense attorneys requested trial before an impartial jury. Will's lawyer was in no hurry to bring his case to court. Juan, however, was being held in jail. Juan's lawyer asked for trial as soon as possible.

★ 8 ★

JUSTICE DURING
THE TRIAL

SUBPOENA OF
DEFENSE WITNESSES

Both Will and Juan had the right to force anyone who could
help their cases to appear during their trial. Their defense
lawyers had only to request that these people be served with
a subpoena. Witnesses, of course, can refuse to testify if their
testimony could *incriminate* them or make them seem guilty
of a crime. In Juan's case, two men had seen him run down
the steps of his apartment building. They knew Juan because
they lived in the neighborhood. Neither wanted to come to
court because they would lose work time, but the subpoena
overrode their objections. Will's lawyer subpoenaed several
important citizens who, not knowing Will was guilty, had
offered to testify about his fine character and honesty.

JURY SELECTION

Since both Juan and Will had the right to a trial by an impartial jury, both the defense and prosecuting attorneys had

some voice in the selection of the jury. They had the right to question potential jurors and excuse those who might be prejudiced against their client's race, religion, or national origin. In the jury selection for Juan's trial, for instance, one juror divulged that his sister had been robbed by a Puerto Rican man three years before. Juan's lawyer thought that he might be predisposed to finding Juan guilty and excluded him. Will's lawyer thought that too many jurors from a poor economic background might sway the jury against Will. He tried to get as many middle-class or wealthy people on the jury as possible.

PRESUMPTION
OF INNOCENCE

The workings of a criminal trial are very complex. Special rules govern the methods both lawyers use to argue their cases. But the most important aspect of any trial is *presumption of innocence*. Obviously, if the government levels charges against someone, it is natural to believe there is good reason to do so. Yet the scales of justice are tipped in the defendant's favor by presumption of innocence. Our justice system is based on the requirement that anyone accused of a crime must be presumed not guilty until proven otherwise. The prosecutor must prepare and present a strong case against the defendant. The prosecutor must prove the defendant did in fact commit the crime. The jury is commanded by the judge to ignore the fact that the defendant has already faced the grand jury, that the prosecutor believes he or she has enough evidence to try the case, and that the defendant may be out on bail.

Strict rules limit the evidence the prosecution may present against the defendant. In Will's case, for instance, had

*A witness examines photographs
that have been entered as evidence
in this Massachusetts trial.*

the police not secured a search warrant, the records Will kept that indicated he was altering his clients' accounts could not have been entered as evidence.

If the defendant has a past record, the prosecutor cannot make the jury aware of it except under very specific circumstances. Juan, for instance, had been caught shoplifting when he was fourteen. The prosecutor could not introduce this fact because it might color the jury's opinion of Juan and affect the presumption of innocence.

A defendant is considered innocent. The burden of proof lies with the prosecutor. No defendant can be forced to testify and no implication of guilt can be drawn from his refusal. Juan's lawyer did not want Juan to testify. He knew that once Juan did, the prosecutor had the right to cross-examine him. Once on the stand, Juan had no right to claim Fifth Amendment privilege—"I refuse to answer because my answer may tend to incriminate me." Juan's lawyer knew that Juan could be easily rattled. He was afraid the prosecutor might anger Juan so much that he might lose his temper. Doing so would not help their case. Will, however, wanted a chance to testify. He believed he could sway the jury in his favor and outsmart the prosecutor. He testified.

THE RIGHT TO CROSS-EXAMINATION

Another basic right of the defendant is to cross-examine accusers. This right is part of the Sixth Amendment. The ability to question witnesses against the defendant is basic to a fair trial. Many convincing witnesses, even those who truly believe they saw what they only think they saw, have lost their believability during questioning by the defense. In

Juan's case, cross-examination of the woman who claimed she saw Juan run from the grocery store won his case. While he drew on the blackboard, Juan's attorney asked her to describe exactly what she had seen. It became evident that she had been too far away to recognize Juan's face and that when the criminal had run from the store, she could only have seen his back. This discovery seriously damaged the prosecutor's case.

BEYOND A
REASONABLE DOUBT

Presumption of innocence also requires that the prosecutor prove, *beyond a reasonable doubt*, that the defendant committed the crime. The judge instructs the jury that if the prosecutor has not done that, if the jury has any nagging doubts about the defendant's guilt, they must give the defendant the benefit of the doubt. This places great responsibility on the prosecutor. If the defense lawyer can point to "facts" that do not add up, if he can show that the prosecutor has drawn faulty conclusions, or that the evidence is incomplete, that constitutes a reasonable doubt. The defendant can be acquitted. In Juan's case, that is exactly what happened. The jury decided that Juan's running down the street just after the crime had been committed could easily have been a coincidence. They disregarded the woman's identification of Juan as the criminal because her story had too many flaws. They had reasonable doubts about Juan's guilt. Juan returned to his family that very day.

The jury had no reasonable doubts about Will's guilt. The prosecutor had presented carefully detailed, fully supported evidence against Will. He had matched disappearances of

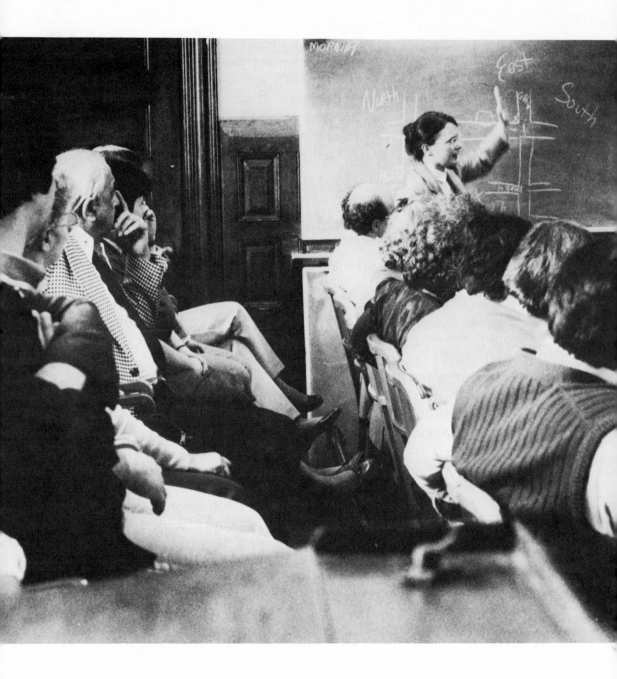

money from client accounts to deposits Will made in his personal bank account. He clearly showed that over a period of three years, Will had systematically embezzled thousands of dollars. The jury found Will guilty. Once again, the judge raised Will's bail, and stated that he would sentence Will the following week.

SENTENCING

Before pronouncing Will's sentence, the judge studied background material that had been gathered about Will. He also considered the maximum and minimum penalties allowed by law for Will's particular crime. He knew that the penalty he imposed could not be "cruel or unusual," but that it must reflect the seriousness of Will's crime. The following week, the judge sentenced Will to five years in the state penitentiary and imposed a fine of $5,000.

If Juan had been found guilty, the judge could have given him the death penalty. The death penalty is not considered cruel or unusual for the crime of murder. Before sentencing, however, the judge would have to carefully consider all the facts related to Juan's "crime." His character and previous record would influence the judge's decision. So would the circumstances surrounding his crime. The death sentence cannot be given to everyone convicted of murder.

Jurors must weigh all the facts and arguments that have been presented, and determine if the prosecution has proved the guilt of the defendant beyond a reasonable doubt.

★ 9 ★

JUSTICE AFTER
SENTENCING

Even though the judge sentenced Will to five years in prison, Will still had the right to appeal his sentence in a higher court. Many times judges in appeals courts will reverse the decisions of lower court judges. Any fault in the way the trial was conducted can lead to such a reversal. The appeals court judge may decide the defendant was denied "due process." A higher court can even rule that a case be retried. Will, however, chose not to appeal his conviction. He was sent directly to the state penitentiary.

Our justice system imprisons those convicted of crimes for several reasons. Prison removes dangerous people from society. If they have already hurt or killed, they may do so again. If they have kidnapped or stolen or embezzled money, they may not be physically dangerous, but they do endanger law and order. Society demands protection from known criminals.

Additionally, revenge, getting even, has been part of humankind's laws since the earliest times. Paying for a crime by doing time in jail is a kind of revenge society imposes on those convicted.

Fines, imprisonment, and execution are also used to set an example. They stand as warnings to others who might be tempted to break the law.

Finally, imprisonment can also be an opportunity to rehabilitate a criminal. While imprisoned, our justice system tries to change a person by teaching that crime does not pay. In the best of our prison systems, opportunities to finish high school or learn a trade are provided so that when a prisoner is released he or she can find a decent job.

In recent years, however, studies have shown that our prison system does little to change criminal behavior. Contact with hard-core criminals often teaches prisoners new ways to beat the system. Prison routine and mistreatment by guards and prison authorities often give the convict more reason to hate the system. At many prisons, conditions are unbearable. Food infested with bugs, unsanitary toilet facilities, and overcrowding are serious problems. Few prisons offer training for high-paying jobs. Few prisons even pay their guards enough to attract the best possible candidates. Rings organized among prisoners make life in prison a terrifying experience. Too often the effect of prison isn't a fear of getting in trouble again. Instead it is a bitter hatred of society.

Will's prison sentence of five years is the maximum amount of time he will be required to serve, unless he gets in more trouble while there. If he can stay out of trouble with other prisoners and the guards, the amount of time he has to serve may be lessened. He will apply for parole, early release from prison, as soon as he is eligible. The parole board will consider his case, his behavior in prison, the recommendation of prison officials, and the likelihood of his staying out of trouble. If parole is not granted on his first try, Will can

continue requests for parole until it is either granted or his sentence has been served.

Once a convict has been paroled, he is responsible to his parole officer, a government employee charged with overseeing the behavior of parolees for a certain amount of time after their release from prison. When Will is paroled, he will have to report to his parole officer weekly. He will bring with him pay stubs to prove he is working. Strict rules govern his behavior while he is on parole. He cannot leave the state without his parole officer's permission. He cannot carry a weapon. He must not get in any trouble. Arrest for another crime could send him straight back to the penitentiary.

Although Will may serve his time and complete his parole successfully, he will always have a record. Many employers' application forms ask whether the applicant has ever been convicted of a felony. Many employers are not willing to take the risk of hiring an ex-con. Other jobs, those that require special licenses, will never be open to him because these licenses are not granted to convicted felons.

Although great strides have been made in protecting the rights of those accused of crimes, very little has been done for those found guilty. To say that those who break the law do not deserve protection is too simple an excuse. The number of convicts who commit other crimes after release from prison is great. Until prison and parole systems change, that figure is not likely to lessen.

A prison sentence is intended both to punish and to rehabilitate. But studies have shown that the current prison system does little to change criminal behavior.

★ 10 ★

CIVIL JUSTICE

When Juan and Will were arrested, they were scheduled for trial in a criminal court. The federal or state government brings someone to trial in a criminal court because he has not only caused an "injury" but has also endangered the peace and order that the public requires. The government, then, represents the people in our justice system. Juan was accused of armed robbery and murder. Will was accused of embezzling money from his clients. People accused of other crimes such as assault, bribery, theft, blackmail and kidnapping also find themselves in a criminal court. The person who was injured has only to sign a complaint. He then becomes the government's chief witness. From that point on, the government takes all the steps necessary to see that justice is done.

Not all "injuries" are criminal. Not all abuses of rights endanger the public good. Far more often, private citizens have disputes with one another over the terms of contracts or the amount of money owed them or the failure of one citizen to honor an agreement. The civil court is the place where these disputes are settled. People who believe they have been injured argue their cases in court and if the court agrees with them, it ensures that they get justice.

In a civil court a citizen who believes his rights have been abused hires a lawyer and fights his own case. He is called the *plaintiff*. He *sues* the person he believes responsible, the *defendant*. This forces the defendant into court.

The responsibility of the judge and jury in a civil court is not to determine guilt and punishment. They must find a fair solution to the problem. Perhaps the owner of a building has failed to live up to his responsibilities to his tenants. Or perhaps a tenant has not paid his rent and the owner wants him evicted. A woman injured in a car accident cannot agree on a fair settlement with the insurance company. A patient believes his doctor's mistakes are responsible for the paralysis of his legs. These are the kinds of cases tried in a civil court.

The judge and jury determine whether the claims made are true and decide how the dispute will be settled. Solutions are often in the form of money paid to the plaintiff. A doctor, for instance, may be ordered to pay his injured patient damages. A parent may be ordered to pay child support. Other times the solution will be an order forbidding the defendant to continue a certain practice such as using another company's name. Sometimes the court will order the defendant to make repairs or furnish heat or complete work on a building or rehire an employee who was fired. If these commands are ignored, the defendant can be fined and, if held in contempt of court, sent to jail. Once the court has made its decision, the government then sees to it that justice is done.

Use of the civil courts to obtain justice has mushroomed in past years. We have become a suing society. Today, more than twelve million suits are brought each year. The courts are so overburdened that the average time necessary to close a case in the federal courts is nineteen months. For state courts, the time is longer.

Sometimes suits are for ridiculous "injuries." A schoolboy sued the company that made a cookie another child had thrown in his eye. Several football fans sued the referee because of a bad call. These cases increase the amount of time it takes for those who do have a valid injury to be heard.

Not only have individual suits buried the courts, but public interest suits have forced the courts to solve numerous social problems. The courts find themselves making public policy, often when the job could be done better by public officials. Some cases involving toxic waste or mining rights, employee relations or zoning issues, could well be disposed of outside of the courts.

Yet the civil courts must always be the place where, all else failing, people can find justice. If someone breaks a contract or misrepresents a product or cheats another, the civil court is the place to make him pay for these injuries. If someone publishes "facts" about another that are untrue and which damage the other's reputation, the civil court can determine that a wrong has been done and decide the amount of damages to be paid. If a landlord or employer discriminates against another because of race, color, religion, or sex, the "victim" has recourse in the courts.

Once the "injured" person, the plaintiff, has contacted a lawyer and the lawyer has agreed to take the case, the lawyer contacts the other party, the defendant. He promises that civil action will be taken if his client's demands are not met. Often this threat is enough to resolve the problem.

If the defendant refuses to settle, the plaintiff then files a complaint with the court. The complaint describes the nature of the charges against the defendant. The complaint and a summons to appear in court are then served on the defendant.

The defendant has ten to sixty days to file an *answer*. In the answer, he may add new "facts" in his defense. If the defendant fails to answer, the plaintiff likely wins the case by default.

The next step is called *discovery*. It is a meeting of both the plaintiff and the defendant in either's lawyer's office. Hundreds of questions must be answered and often this step takes months to complete. All testimony is recorded by a court stenographer. Evidence such as letters or photographs may be requested. No requested evidence can be withheld. To do so is considered contempt of court, which is punishable. Discovery gives both sides the oppportunity to see the case against them. Many cases are resolved after discovery because, having a truer picture of their chances in the courtroom, plaintiffs and defendants decide it is cheaper or safer to do so.

Before cases actually go to court, nearly ninety percent of them are dropped or settled. Once in court, civil trials are very much like criminal trials. Jurors are selected if a jury trial is demanded. The plaintiff presents his case. The defendant's lawyer cross-examines. The defendant presents his case. Both sides sum up, after which the jury decides. Either side can appeal the jury's verdict to a higher court.

Criminal courts provide the mechanism to see to it that the rights of anyone accused of a crime are preserved. They limit the power of government, seeing to it that government protects what it is empowered to protect without going beyond the boundaries of the Constitution and the Bill of Rights. Criminal courts also punish those who victimize others. Civil courts provide the mechanism to settle disputes peaceably. They see to it that the rights of the people are not abused, that all are treated fairly, and that all can use the power of the law to get justice when it is denied them. Both criminal and civil courts are essential if true justice is ever to be achieved.

★ 11 ★

HOW JUST IS
OUR SYSTEM OF
JUSTICE?

A perfect justice system clearly and completely defines and protects the rights of each individual. Such a system ensures that every person is treated fairly. No matter who a person is, no matter how rich or poor, no matter what his race, religion, national origin, or sex, he or she can expect to be treated as well as any other person. A perfect justice system does not consider whether one *deserves* justice. The rights, privileges, and protections of its laws are given to its criminals as well as its honest, law-abiding citizens.

A perfect system of justice, on the other hand, clearly and completely defines and protects the rights of the group, the people, and the government the people have set up. It protects all people and their government from those who try to destroy it. It maintains peace and order, and punishes those who undermine peace and order. A true justice system is the power of the group, the people, to limit what individuals may and may not do by defining what is legal and illegal. It also limits those who might otherwise abuse others' rights.

Balancing the rights of the individual and the rights of the group is no easy task. To achieve perfect balance is probably impossible. That is why no system of justice ever designed has been perfect.

For most of humankind's history, the needs and rights of the group, the government, or the select few who run the government have been more important than the needs or rights of any single individual. Because of that, the history of justice details abuse of the poor or the powerless. With the coming of democratic ideals, however, the rights of the individual grew more and more important. If each and every individual did not have definite rights and some power that protected those rights, democracy could not exist. That is why our forebears thought and argued so long and so hard as they wrote both our Constitution and our Bill of Rights. They knew how important it was to prevent the powerful from mistreating the powerless. They knew also how necessary a strong government was to maintaining peace and order. They recognized the difficulty in creating a perfect balance.

Our justice system is not perfect. During the 1960s, those who fought for civil rights showed Americans many of the ways our system failed the individual. In an effort to balance the system, some believe justice began to favor the rights of the individual over the group. The Miranda Warning and new search and seizure laws, for instance, seemed to make catching and punishing criminals more and more difficult. Some said we had handcuffed our police and given the jail-cell key to our criminals.

Recently, the public has been dismayed and angered by growing crime rates. Our justice system seems unable to keep criminals off the streets. This has led to new "get tough" policies in the courts—stiffer sentences and speedier trials for repeat offenders, those constantly in trouble with the law. Like the pendulum on a clock, our justice system seems to go a little too far one way and then a little too far the other.

What is important, however, is that our system is not rigid. It can change. The feelings of the people are reflected in those changes. Citizens, lawyers, judges, and juries constantly reevaluate, reinterpret, change or modify what the law means. Yet they always do so with an eye to our Constitution and Bill of Rights. The Constitution and Bill of Rights ensure that changes never go beyond their original meaning and limits.

Certainly our system has flaws. Too much of the justice we expect and get is left to chance. Whether one is arrested depends upon individual police officers. Whether one is charged depends on individual prosecutors. The charge itself depends on plea bargaining. How a trial is run depends on how good a lawyer one has and how fair the judge is. The verdict depends on the jury. The punishment depends on the laws of the state or city in which the crime was committed.

The answer to how just is our system of justice, then, cannot be given on the basis of how perfect it is. It can never be perfect. The answer must be based on how alive it is. Is it a growing, changing, healthy system? Or is it stale, decaying, dying, or dead?

We have lower courts that every day give interpretation to the law. Every day lawyers and judges argue and evaluate its meaning. Every day decisions are made that further define the rights of all.

We have higher courts and appeals courts. There, every day other lawyers and other judges examine decisions that have been made, reversing those that are not just or that are not within the power of the law.

The current Justices of the Supreme Court,
the highest court in the country: (left to right)
John Paul Stevens, Thurgood Marshall,
William H. Rehnquist, Byron R. White,
Harry A. Blackmun, William J. Brennan, Jr.,
Warren E. Burger, Sandra Day O'Connor,
and Lewis F. Powell, Jr.

Finally, we have the Supreme Court of the United States. It is the most powerful court in our country. The Supreme Court, composed of some of our wisest and most experienced judges, has the final say in what justice means and how it is to be applied. Their responsibility is to weigh the sides of disputes that involve the rights of the individual and the rights of the group. Theirs is the final responsibility to interpret and define the meaning of our Constitution and Bill of Rights.

Is our justice system alive? Unquestionably so. Is it growing and changing, so that it meets new needs? It grows and changes every day. Is it healthy? Compare the rights we have today to those of our earliest history. Or those of British commoners in the eighth or tenth century. Or to those who lived under Puritan rule in Colonial America. Or even to those Americans before the Civil War who were slaves. Or to poor, uneducated Americans before the right to a public defender in all cases involving jail sentences was established. Our justice system is most certainly healthy.

Why is it healthy? First of all, the founders of our country gave us the seeds to build a healthy justice system in both the Constitution and our Bill of Rights. But just having the seeds was not enough. As with any living thing, our justice system had to be cared for to grow strong. It had to be protected from the weeds that could strangle it—by guarding against laws or court decisions that might change or destroy the original meaning of the Constitution and the Bill of Rights. It had to be protected from the drought of narrow minds or those with selfish motives. It had to be watered with the constant attention of citizens determined to see justice done. It needed the sunlight of great minds weighing the meaning of laws and balancing individual rights and group safety.

It still needs time to grow. It is not yet fully mature. It must be protected from disease or pests by Americans who realize that justice means protection of ourselves, each and every one of us. The abuse of any citizen's rights, the denial of justice to any one citizen, even if he is a criminal, can in the long run destroy that protection we have worked so hard to achieve.

INDEX